He Loves Me,

He Loves Me NOT

Tips and tools for distinguishing between

Love, and its counterfeit – Lust

He Loves Me,

He Loves Me NOT

Tips and tools for distinguishing between

Love, and its counterfeit – Lust

He Loves Me,

He Loves Me NOT

Tips and tools for distinguishing between

Love, and its counterfeit – Lust

LaWanda Montgomery

DESTINY

Destiny House Publishing, LLC

He Loves Me, He Loves Me NOT

Tips and Tools for Distinguishing Love, from its Counterfeit - Lust

Published by Destiny House Publishing, LLC

Copyright ©2013 LaWanda Montgomery

ISBN- 978-193686775 2

Unless otherwise stated, all scripture quotations are from the Holy Bible, King James Version. Scripture references that do not have the Bible version noted are the author's paraphrase.

Cover design and Publication Layout: RL Smith Designs

Artwork from Dreamstime

Editing: Destiny House Publishing, LLC

Printed in the United States of America

For information:

Destiny House Publishing, LLC

www.destinyhousepublishing.com

Email: inquiry@destinyhousepublishing.com

P.O. Box 19774 Detroit, MI 48219 888-890-9455

Contents

Acknowledgements

There are quite a few people I'd like to acknowledge in this book. I must start off by acknowledging my Husband, Father, Brother and Friend, Jesus Christ.. Thank You Lord for rebirthing my zeal and desire to write; somehow I'd lost it along the way. I love You Lord!

Second, I'd like to acknowledge my daughter LaShara. I am so very grateful to be your mother and I pray that I can be all that you deserve. You are growing to be such a beautiful young lady both inside and out. More importantly you have chosen on your own to serve The Lord, and I pray that you will allow Him to forever keep you!
I know it may seem a little weird to learn of some of the details that you had not yet heard of in the relationship of your father and I. Prayerfully there's nothing too hard for you to learn of, and our story will be used to help you or someone else one day. I love you daughter!

Next, I'd like to acknowledge my parents, (Mom- Debra, and Dad- Charles) who have been a great help to me both during the actual turn of events, as well as now. I pray that you will understand that everything in the story is a depiction of how I interpreted things as a young adult and there is truly nothing but love and respect for you as I stand today. God has healed and renewed my heart and way of thinking and for that I am grateful! I love you Mom and Dad!

I'd also like to thank my family and friends, including my Greater Works Family, for loving and pushing me to complete this journey.

My Spiritual Leaders, Apostle Oscar and Prophetess Crystal Jones, Elder Cleave Davis and Elder Joceline Bronson, I thank you for the encouragement to seek God for my gifts.
I love you all!

Can't forget about my other Spiritual Mom, Joyce Meyer (though I don't know you personally,) I truly thank God for your life and ministry! Not sure where I'd be if I hadn't been presented with your cassette tapes and books years ago. I thank God for you!

Lastly, I thank that special someone who allowed me to share a piece of our story with the world. I believe that this story and the stories we have yet to tell will greatly benefit many, as God will use our testimony to help others! I must also acknowledge you as the reason for my miracle, and greatest accomplishment thus far, our daughter LaShara.
I love and appreciate you tremendously!

Dedication

This book is dedicated to every young lady and woman, who has unfortunately found, still finds, or at some point will find, herself in a mirror crying and wondering how I got here. It seems to be quite common for women at some point in their lives, to be in a place of pain and confusion when they find that they have lost love.

"How could he do this to me, I thought he loved me?"
"What happened to our relationship, we were so in love?"

Unfortunately the answers to these questions are usually not what we anticipate or hope to hear, and instead involves the revelation of truth. The truth that there was never really any love in the first place. It was all an illusion, lust camouflaged as love and deceiving both or at least one of the involved parties.

If this is you, and you're wondering what to do now, my heart and prayers are with you. There is a better day ahead, but it must begin with the understanding and acceptance of truth.

Allow Truth to heal your brokenness and introduce you to Love.

Love Heals!

Introduction

I can remember exactly where I was and what I was doing when God revealed to me that the marriage I'd spent countless hours praying and fasting for was based on a foundation of no more than sin. As I sat reading of a young lady who'd mistaken the lust she had in a relationship, for love, it happened. God revealed the same was true of many relationships, including my own.

"Lust, how could this apply to me Lord, after all, we were married?" My heart dropped, my mind raced, and I instantly began to sob. What type of fool have I been all these years? I KNOW I love him, so is it that You're telling me he never loved me? Lord are You telling me my whole marriage has been a big lie? All these questions and more began to flood my mind. It was hard to accept at first but I later realized I'd been entangled in a world of witchcraft and lust and had no idea. After all, in my mind, lust was one of the more "obvious" sins. Lust had a way of revealing itself in every conversation and was evident in the way a person walked or in their choice of clothing. Lust is purely a sexual sin, right? Not so...

I believe that God will use this book to help shed light on this myth. Lust is far more deceitful and destructive than one would think. It does not necessarily have to do with ones desire to have sex or even be sexually involved. One can lust for a car, a talent or gifting, money, and as I am now learning, *one can lust for love*. The danger of it is, until you begin to learn of God, Who IS love, you can easily be fooled into believing that the relationship you have is solid and based on a foundation of, or has finally evolved into love.

My prayer is that by the end of this reading, God will have revealed to every reader the truth behind their desires and the foundation of their relationships. God wants for us to be healthy and whole in every area and if we have developed relationships of lust, we are sure to experience immense heartache as they are certain to crumble.

Psalms 127:1 - Unless the Lord builds the house, its builders labor in vain.

"The house" in this case, is synonymous with a relationship or marriage. Because God loves us so much, He will not allow us to be fooled by the enemy's devices, and lust is a device of the enemy!

If in a relationship, God may remove the person from our lives entirely once we decide to give Him our lives and live a lifestyle of holiness and righteousness. However if you've entered into a marriage based solely on lust, God still honors this covenant, but will likely allow the marriage to dismantle, in which He will rebuild it with love as the new foundation.

I know firsthand what it's like to have this happen, to have a seemingly good thing going and add God to the mix only to have everything fall apart soon thereafter. For many years I was confused and cried out to God about this. When things got really dark for me, I would even accuse God for my relationship falling apart, and though I may have never said it aloud, it rang ever so loudly in my heart!

Before I met God, I was in a relationship with the father of my child for years, knowingly living in sin, and not because I'd been raised in the church and been saved all my life, but because there seemed to always be an aunt, a co-worker, or maybe even just an older married couple who'd see the three of us at a restaurant and lecture us on getting things right with God by getting married. "God doesn't want His children playing house and shacking up", was the resounding message we'd hear seemingly everywhere we'd go, nevertheless we were comfortable. Sure we had our problems, but we had "good" jobs, a house, a new car (for me) and even a conversion van (for him); and did I mention our dog Kiss and cat Heather?

More importantly we were soul mates; we loved each other and had a family. Considering we'd never seen our parents interact for more than a few minutes at a time, let alone live together with all the fixings, we felt as if we had something really special. Of course, we'd discuss marriage from time to time, but it wasn't something that either of us felt we needed to rush into. But with every reminder that we were "shacking," and every announcement of taking the next step toward marriage by my friends and peers, I began to feel inadequate. I would mentally entertain the idea that maybe I was one of the cows giving out free milk, never to be purchased. With every Word of truth spoken on one of the many Gospel tapes lent to me from co-workers, or from the many churches I visited, the danger of fornication began to concern me. Marriage seemed to be the only way to remedy these nagging feelings.

I can't describe it with words but there is an ever so present nudging felt in your spirit when God is in pursuit of you. This nudging became impossible for me to ignore after a while, so I made the decision to begin my search for a church home. During this time I decided to agree with God and receive the call of salvation which also meant I'd made the decision to change my life, and no longer live in sin with Brandon, but to get married. The tricky part was I forgot this was a decision that would require two people, so of course this is when the "witchcraft" began. Though he'd join me at church from time to time, Brandon had yet to receive the call of salvation but I was saved and "holy" now and therefore everybody in my house would need to fall in line too! Our late night pillow talk sessions about one day getting married, having more children, and buying our dream home, became "Nigga you don't think we about to be having sex and laying up and we not married right? You need to quit talking about it and be about it! We ain't gone be shacking up and living in sin for life! I mean how long you think I'm gone live in this neighborhood, I'm ready to move, I want a baby", and so on and so on. He'd soon become regularly subjected to a full scale nagging session packed with rejection and manipulation, which became the catalyst, and unfortunate chain of events leading to me getting what I wanted, the proposal, the ring, and finally his last name, some courtship huh?

Looking back on it now, it is evident that our relationship immediately began to dismantle once I'd received Christ as my Savior! God began to expose the root of our problems and the foundation of our relationship, not because God didn't want me to be happy, but because God loved me enough to reveal truth! He wanted to order my steps from glory to glory and faith to faith. There was no way God would've been glorified in the relationship I was in when I'd gotten saved. Not only were we guilty of sinning, as we all are, but we were living lives of sin. The mere fact that I'd decided to now dress my sin up in an "I do" didn't change the fact that there was a stronghold of lust and sexual sin in our lives; it simply changed "clothes" from fornication to now adultery.

The spirit of lust that we were entertaining was never satisfied and seemingly became all the more greedy after marriage. It grew bigger and changed forms several times causing us to further taint God's design for marriage. The Word of God describes the marriage bed as undefiled, and because of this, many believe that it means anything goes as long as you're married. Not so! When God made this declaration, He didn't plan for us to interpret this as sexual sin is acceptable as long as you're married and using the sin to please your mate! God never intended and will not allow us to skew His perfect institution of marriage with unholy addictions and practices such as the use of pornography for entertainment, and the sin of homosexuality which takes place when lust decides sex would be far more enjoyable when including another person; this is sexual immorality at its height!

My journey from swearing off relationships to finding and falling head over heels in love with my assumed "soul mate" has been captured in the next several pages of this book.

After going through a gut wrenching break up and what appeared to be the end of the world with Daniel, a guy I'd met in my first year of high school, and raked over the coals by several others prior to him, (and all this occurring at the tender age of 14), I'd closed off my heart and swore to never allow myself to endure the pain I'd felt with him again. I'd made a mental note to self that it would be a miracle if I ever found or allowed myself to "love" again. This next guy would have to be a true present day knight in shining armor who'd sweep me off my feet by being all that Daniel was and more. Besides I was getting a fresh new start at a new school and I'd have no time to involve myself with the nonsense that accompanied dating, or so I thought.

Brandon & Dianna

Chapter 1

I was 15 when I met my husband, Brandon. The two of us attended the same high school together for a semester at Hadley High. I transferred schools during the second semester of my sophomore year, and enrolled in the neighborhood high school. Day one greeted me with several familiar faces both seemingly happy and indifferent of my arrival. Choosing my schedule of classes posed somewhat of a challenge seeing as how I'd spent so much of my previous semester suspended and earned no credit hours. Where would I begin, I thought? Would there be a way to salvage my sophomore year? I was overjoyed after meeting my school counselor who reassured me that I would be just fine as long as I was willing to work hard. She smiled and gave me my new schedule and other necessary tools for a successful transition. She then directed me to the school's auditorium for a short assembly in which I would be introduced to the school's principal and several other faculty members. I could've never in a million years have imagined that this very assembly would also be the place where I'd be introduced to my future husband and father of my child, but so it was.

The room was full from wall to wall with restless teenagers who became louder by the minute. They eventually began to entertain themselves with a ruthless game of dodge ball using the papered balls they'd assembled with pages from the school's newsletter, as we waited for the schools administrators to arrive. Though I hadn't chosen to join in, it wasn't long before I became a victim of the papered artillery. As I went to pick the ball up from where it had bounced from me and onto the floor, just as in the movies, I was met eye to eye by one of the finest guys I'd ever seen. He was tall, with a caramel complexion and nicely built; not too slim, and not too husky but just right. Quickly grabbing the paper up and launching it across the room seemingly unfazed by its final destination, he then said, "Excuse these clowns in here. You need any help, I got you li'l lady." We both smiled as he reached out his hand and introduced himself as B.

"B"? I asked.

"Yes," he answered. "My real name is somewhat hard to pronounce, it's French."

"Okay, well it's nice to meet you B, I'm Dianna." Shortly thereafter the administrators arrived quickly demanding the attention of the overcrowded auditorium, and away he went.

After leaving the assembly, I hadn't really thought too much about the encounter with B. Besides, he was obviously older than me, which meant we probably wouldn't have any classes together, and besides that, there was no way he hadn't already been claimed by the token beauty and captain of the cheer team I assumed. However I'd run into him in the hallways, and from time to time in the lunchroom, and I'd try my best to ensure that I cross every "t" and dot every "i" for the encounter. I'd begin by shellacking on layers of lip gloss. Then I'd douse myself in perfume, and as if the already tight jeans that gave the appearance of being painted on weren't doing enough to advertise my curves, I'd be sure to accentuate the positive by adding a spine jerking switch to my walk. I'd never say much, but I could always count on B to provoke a dialogue between us. He kept me smiling with his flirtatious demeanor and laughing as he was sure to bring along with him, a host of jokes and quick wit to address me. He had to be one of the funniest people I knew, and still is! He was also one of the more well put together guys I knew, that is other than my dad, and there was a refreshing and confident air about him that was captivating to say the least.

Chapter 2

Adorned in his crisply pressed Ralph Lauren button up and accompanying slacks, his Gucci loafers never seemed to touch the floor as he appeared to float while walking the halls of Hadley. We'd always be sure to say hello and maybe even have a few quick words with one another in passing, but there was something vastly different about the vibe between us on this particular day. We said our "hey how you doing's" but as I turned to continue down the hall, he called my name and gestured for me to come back to him, and I did, only to be gifted with a warm smile and request for a hug. As I agreed to his request, I'd become overwhelmed by this new dimension we seemingly had entered together. I felt as if I were going to melt away right there in that very spot!

Wow! His arms, his scent, his embrace was like none I'd experienced before, but nevertheless I was sure to play it cool as we released each other, and walked our separate ways, or at least I thought I kept my cool. I made it to class just in time to avoid the tardy bell as it rang for the start of my 4th period class. I'd been doing well in all my classes and wanted to keep it that way. I truly couldn't afford another failed semester.

The remainder of the day was fairly difficult for me as I was in a daze following that breathtaking hug I'd shared with B. Yet I was able to make it through the class and before long the day was over. As I reflected on the encounter from earlier, I began to feel embarrassed that I'd gotten so worked up about a simple hug, and vowed to make every effort to avoid him from that day on. After all, he was a senior and would be graduating soon so I should be able to pull it off I thought, and I'd almost been successful.

With just a week left in the school year, I was chosen by one of my teachers to run an errand. Hall pass in hand, I headed down the back stairway and was pleasantly surprised to run into none other than my heartthrob. "Hey B," I shouted as I attempted to quickly continue down the stairs to complete the assigned errand, and more importantly to avoid B.

"Slow down. Where are you going? I guess you just don't have no time to kick it with ya boy no more huh?"

"Oh, I'm sorry; it's just that Mr. Brown sent me to…" He cut me off by handing me an envelope.

"What's this?" I asked as I looked down at it, he began to write on it his name and phone number.

"Call me sometimes, don't be a stranger," he said as he continued up the stairs.

I stood there for a moment in amazement thinking, I can't believe I let him do it again, meaning leave me giddy and goofy eyed, and all the more excited to see that he'd actually written down his full name, "Brandon Anderson."

Chapter 3

The school year ended on a great note for me, but unfortunately I was one of the "lucky" teenagers with no plans for the summer vacation. The summer job I worked last year was no longer an option. I hadn't found another to replace it, so I didn't have very high hopes for anything except the opportunity to sleep my days away; awaking only to eat and watch my daytime soap operas and talk shows. Well, there was driver's training in a few weeks, but that would be the highlight of my summer. Bored and insistent upon finding something to do, I began to sort through a few things in my room. I stumbled across the infamous envelope; not that I'd misplaced it. I'd done everything short of frame it in hopes of preserving it. It was nearly three weeks since I'd seen or heard from Brandon, but I had yet to muster up the courage to call him. Besides, what would I say? What if he doesn't answer?

Worse still, what if his mother answers? Did he really want to talk to me anyway? Would he even remember who I was? What would we talk about? How do I pronounce his name, "Brandon," doesn't seem like anything French to me? I'd undergone this very line of questioning off and on for three weeks now and decided that today would be the day, enough is enough already, after all it's just a phone call I thought. Anyhow, who was I kidding I was terrified so I neatly refolded the envelope in the exact squares it was when B pulled it from his pocket to hand it to me, and placed it back between the blank pages of my diary.

Palms sweaty and heart racing, I sat with the phone in one hand and the envelope in the other. I'd start to dial his number and then I'd hang up. I picked up the phone again and even though we both lived in the same city and had the same area code, to prolong things this time I decided I'd dial the area code first along with six of the remaining seven numbers. Eyes tightly squeezed and finger over the four, I squealed in embarrassment and pressed down. I couldn't believe what I'd just done and I quickly lifted my thumb from the four and replaced it over the disconnect button. I repeated this several times but on the last attempt, I sat frozen with anticipation. I'd made the decision to allow it to ring this time, but "no more than two times" I said aloud, when I heard the first ring. Okay, it's too late to hang up now, but I will only allow it to ring once more and then I will hang up. Just as I finished my thought, the third ring was quickly shortened by a male voice, "Hello?"

My mind and heart raced a million miles a minute! Oh man, was that him? After all I'd never heard his "phone voice". I couldn't believe I was doing this. What will I say? If I say, "Hello, may I speak to Brandon?" and this *is* Brandon, I will sound foolish!

"Hello?" the voice repeated.

"Hello, may I speak to Brandon please?"

"Speak to who?" he asked, triggering yet another marathon between my heart and mind. With that questionable response, I began to wonder if I'd pronounced his name correctly, or worse, if Brandon had purposefully given me the wrong number. Or was it that I sounded crazy for requesting to speak to Brandon when I already was? I followed by repeating slightly louder than the first time, "Hello, may I speak with Brandon please?"

"Oh, you want to speak to B? He's not here right now, may I ask who's calling?"

"This is his friend, Dianna from school. Will you let him know I called please?"

"Okay Dianna, I will give him the message to call you." And with that, three weeks of fear had been extinguished. But just as I pressed the button to disconnect, it registered that the gentleman on the other line said he'd tell B to call me, but I never gave B my number. How would he call me back? Will I have to endure the stress of that first call again, "good grief,"

I mumbled with my best Charlie Brown impression, and soon thereafter I'd drifted off to sleep.

My afternoon nap was cut short as I was awakened by the ringing of the cordless phone that I'd obviously never released after the call, because it was still in my hand. I cleared my throat and answered, "Hello?" Imagine my surprise when the voice on the other line replied, "Hello, may I speak with Dianna please?" Heart pounding, I sheepishly responded, "This is she, who's calling?"

"Hey, Dianna this is B, I just got home and my brother told me you called for me."

"Yeah, I did, but I'll admit, I wasn't expecting you to call me back. How'd you get my number?"

"I looked through the names on the caller ID box, saw your last name, and called you back. I hoped this was the right number. By the way, I'm not going to get you in any trouble for calling am I?"

"Oh no, it's fine, I was just wondering," I said, astonished that this "caller ID" thing really worked. I'd heard about it but never knew anyone who'd actually had one in their home. "How are you?" I asked.

"I'm great now", he responded. "I was beginning to think you were never going to call me."

Wow! He actually thought about me, and was concerned with whether or not I would call? Sad to say, but I was all in from that point; hook, line, and sinker. Infatuation had its grip, and turning back was no longer an option for me. Even sadder to say, it didn't take much time after the initial phone call before I became sexually involved with him, and soon thereafter, pregnant with our child.

Chapter 4

I kept my head down and eyes closed in an effort to avoid the look of pain and disappointment on my mother's face as the nurse drew blood and asked several embarrassing questions regarding my sex life.

"So Dianna, Are you sexually active?"

"Not really," I replied, though I had been with B just two days prior. Nevertheless, her interrogation continued.

"Well, have you had sex before and if so with how many partners?"

This completely annoyed me and I'm assuming my mother as well.

"Well maybe if I leave the room she'll answer your questions," my mom answered.

"You don't have to leave," I said with my mouth as my heart and mind screamed, YES, PLEASE LEAVE! The annoying nurse reiterated the same,

"Yes, Miss Martin, you don't have to leave, seeing as how she is still a minor it is totally up to you."

At that, I was livid! Was she trying to change this simple doctor's visit (discomfort during urination), to an emergency room visit for my cracked skull? Why was she asking me about sex anyway? Aren't I here because I'm in pain and not because I had a request for birth control? As my mother left the room, the nurse began to go even harder on me, "Now come on Dianna; you already know these test we're taking are probably going to tell the story for you. So you may as well speak for yourself. I've seen this too many times to ignore the signs and I'm willing to bet a pretty penny you're pregnant."

WHAT? Pregnant, where'd she get that from? I didn't say anything about a missed period or morning sickness, and besides, I told her "not really" when she asked about sex. I sat quietly in front of her, but my mind had a lot more to say, "Please let this test come back negative," I repeated in my head.

"Okay Dianna, I'll leave it at that, she said. Good luck to you sweetie," and she closed the door behind herself.

How'd I get here I wondered as I sat on the table at the doctor's office. I mean true, I'd missed a few doses of my birth control, but I was certain to double up every time that would happen. And yes B and I had only used protection the first few times, but he assured me we were careful and had nothing to worry about. I allowed myself to become falsely secured by these facts and just as I began to calm down and reach out for the Jet magazine I'd brought along from the waiting room, the doctor returned to the room and shouted, "Ok

Dianna, from the looks of all your test results, you appear to have a slight bladder infection..."
YES, I thought, a bladder infection sounds more like… I was cut off by the doctor as he continued,
"…and you're definitely pregnant, any ideas of how far along you might be," he asked.
The volume of the doctor's announcement spared me the discomfort of having to tell my mother, but how in the world would I tell everyone else. I went down the checklist of people who would need to know and became sick to my stomach. Most girls would probably worry about their fathers, but my dad and I weren't that close, I'd be able to get away with a baby or two without him noticing, but what about my grannies, they will be devastated, I thought! I'd began my eleventh grade year at Hadley and seemed to have a good rapport with most my teachers. How would I tell them and what'll they think of me after hearing this? But the biggest fear came when I remembered I had yet to break the news to B that he would soon be a father.

Chapter 5

"Well, Brandon, I have to tell you something and please don't be mad at me," I added. "I think I'm pregnant," completely omitting the fact that I had already taken a test and received confirmation.

"I knew it," he said. "I could tell by the way you've been acting lately." I assumed he was eluding to the fact that I'd began avoiding him by not returning his calls, or I'd take his calls, but made each of our conversations as brief as possible. Or perhaps the fact that I'd deny him the opportunity to see me or pick me up for school for the past few weeks was the giveaway.

"Anyway", he added, "I think we both knew the day it happened, I knew it and I could see in your face that you did too."

He was right. I had an overwhelming sensation to come over me, one that I'd certainly never experienced before but somehow I knew it was far greater than anything sexual, it was almost divine. I don't know, I can't really describe it in words, but I knew the instant it happened, I just tried to ignore it.

It was mid- October and by this time B and I had made the decision that we simply weren't ready to have a child. I was still in high school and he'd recently began taking a few classes for a trade; which meant neither of us had a job or were able to provide for a baby. Well Brandon somehow always seemed to have money, but I certainly didn't feel confident enough to depend on that. After all, I'd always been taught the concept of "momma's baby, daddy's maybe," basically meaning that it would always be up to a woman to provide for the children because most men weren't reliable in these situations. Well for that matter, men weren't really reliable at all from my experience. My father would do what he could but that wasn't often and my mother seemingly never had a man around for longer than a few months at a time. The only man I knew I could depend on was my granddad and his role was limited to say the least. So with these things in mind I'd made the decision to do the unthinkable again, and I'd given B the assignment of coming up with the money for the procedure.

"Brandon, I can't have this baby if we can't come together and figure out a way to take care of it."
"You're right. I don't know anything about taking care of a baby either, so I will do what I can to come up with the money."

"Well, I added, I'm not sure how far along I am and I've been calling around and the price seems to go up with each week of pregnancy so…" He cut me off.

"I will take care of it baby don't worry about it."
"Okay, because I have decided that if I'm still pregnant by Thanksgiving, I will have to tell the rest of my family, seeing as how I'm already starting to get bigger and it's only October."

"I'll take care of it, he repeated."

Thanksgiving came and went with no word from Brandon about the money or the procedure. He never mentioned it and neither did I for that matter. I began to grow accustomed to the new bulge in my lower belly and had begun to fantasize about starting a family with Brandon. Somehow his silence and disregard for any further details about the procedure spoke to me as the sign that he didn't want to follow through with the abortion any longer either and perhaps had begun to have similar fantasies of a family together. That is until the reality of the situation set in. Prenatal visits and baby talk became the center of our, or should I say my conversations, and now it was no longer me being distant and cutting conversations short, but him. We'd still spend time together but not nearly as much as we used to and the vibe between us had seemingly become so heavy and serious. Our carefree, laugh till we cried, get up and go spirit was slowly becoming a thing of the past. Life was real now. Nothing was funny or cute about having a baby at seventeen, neither was it for him at nineteen. Our relationship had to somehow transform into a partnership of sorts and it was evident in the way he looked at me. There was very rarely a look of thrill and passion between us anymore; it had been replaced by an air of responsibility and fear.

Chapter 6

Our baby girl Brionna was beautiful, and had quickly stolen the hearts of all that saw her. I was so elated to finally see that she had made it into the world and was healthy. This somehow served as confirmation for me that I'd done at least one thing right by her, and that I could forgive myself for all the bad decisions and stressing I'd done throughout the pregnancy. I mean if it wasn't one thing it was another, between fights with family, the glances and whispers as I walked the halls at school, and of course the fear of Brandon bailing out on me. I was in constant fight or flight mode, but I was determined, and this determination gave me the drive needed to make it through the entire forty weeks, without ever missing a prenatal visit nor a day of school, and her beautiful and healthy little soul made me proud.

Though it wasn't immediate, I will never forget the day I saw Brandon become a "daddy," of course he was always Brionna's father, but in my opinion, the term "father" was for legalities and technicalities, and a "daddy" was more or less about relationship and intimacy between a father and child. It melted my heart when I saw him look at her, "Wow! I have a daughter," he said as tears begin to well up in his eyes.

I believe she felt it too because she smiled and placed her hand on his face. The moment was so adorable and so very precious. The exchange was brief but sweet and seemed to catapult our relationship from the awkward state of fear and confusion we'd been in for the past several months, into one of like-mindedness and oneness. When it came to our daughter we shared the same views and vowed to do all that we could to be the parents we never had. Before long, we were living in the same home and raising our little Brionna together, and this is where things between us really began to intensify.

Can't remember much about the details of the card, but the one thing I knew rang out the loudest from the pages of it were the words "LOVE Brandon." I couldn't believe what I was seeing and reread it several times to ensure I hadn't imagined it. The infamous word "love" read again on the huge heart held in the hands of the life sized teddy bear which read "I LOVE YOU". He'd given it to me to accompany the card, and with this, I was assured, he must love me. Before this, we hadn't spoken much to each other about our feelings for one another; though I'm sure for him it was evident that I'd began to develop feelings for him and they seemed to grow stronger with each encounter between us. He'd opened that door and for me, there was no turning back. We'd begin to throw the word around at every opportunity, when we would wake up, before we'd end a phone conversation, before, during and after sex, you name it. Though there were fights and situations where we'd do things to betray this love of one another, we had a good thing going for several years before things begin to go haywire. He'd fallen off into sexual encounters with other women and to get back at him I tried unsuccessfully to do the same with various men. I was never able to quite "go there" with another man, instead, I'd become cold and difficult to get along with. I would shut him out and tear him down whenever and however I could as a way of repaying him for the pain I felt from the betrayal. I'd begin to make daily request that he live up to the promises he made to our family by leaving these random women out of our lives and finally making things official between us. However by now, we'd both adopted these insatiable appetites for more, more, more! We were never satisfied no matter how much the other would do to please, we'd always want more.

Besides the fact that I was constantly nagging B about going through with his decision to marry me, we seemed to be consistently bombarded by family and friends suggesting that we stop "shacking up," and make things official, and if not them, co-workers; and as a result he finally followed through. I must say, it was a complete shock to me when he walked through the doors with a huge smile on his face, and the paperwork needed to begin the licensing and certification process in hand. The even bigger surprise came when he dropped to one knee before Brionna, his mother and I and popped the big question, "Dianna, will you marry me?" It wasn't long after that before we'd actually gone down to our city-county building to complete the mission. In a less than intimate setting, we were accompanied by approximately ten other couples of which most seemed to have the look of fear in their eyes that I had in my heart. "What was I doing here?" After looking over to Brandon for reassurance, I was sadly met by the same look of fear and desperation to run for the nearest exit, in his eyes. Nonetheless, we went through with the ceremony, and exchanged vows. Another indication of my lack of preparation was displayed by my inability to provide him with a ring during the ring and vow exchange. However in an effort to satisfy the lust and desires of our flesh, we gave in to it; we gave our flesh exactly what it wanted in order to keep each other content for a while. But as we know, flesh is NEVER satisfied, it always craves for more than what it has. The craving of my flesh eventually led us to get married. I wanted more than the "girlfriend and baby mama title," I wanted to be his wife. The craving of his flesh eventually led us to divorce in order to satisfy his desire to have as many women as he'd like and not be bound to "paperwork" and a discontented wife.

Where Did We Go Wrong?

Chapter 7

Where did we go wrong? Better yet, how did we get here in the first place? The answer is simple: the lust of the flesh, the lust of the eyes, and the pride of life, all of which are used by the enemy to entice the people of God to sin against Him. When we choose these things, we choose to love the world and the things of this world, more than God.

1 John 2:15-16 (NIV) says, "Do not love the world or anything in the world. If anyone loves the world, love for the Father is not in them. For everything in the world- the lust of the flesh, the lust of the eyes, and the pride of life-comes not from the Father but from the world."

In order to better understand this, I will briefly describe what is meant by a few of the terms used. *Lust* refers to the emotional force that is directly associated with the thinking or fantasizing about one's desire.

When I speak of "*lust of flesh*" I am referring to craving for the things of this natural world. Desiring to have something or someone so bad that you are no longer concerned about whether or not this thing is good for you or worse still, displeasing to God.

"The lust of the eyes" refers to the intense desire I had for those things that I saw others with and even the lust I had for the things I hoped to see for B, myself, and our daughter Brionna. As stated in one of the earlier chapters, once I became pregnant with Brionna, I'd begun to fantasize about having a family with Brandon. I found myself mesmerized by these thoughts and eventually did everything in my power to ensure that my desire would come to fruition.

"The pride of life" came into play when I began to esteem myself in high regard because as a married woman, I felt that I'd defeated the odds when it came to teenage girls who become pregnant and eventually become single parents. I didn't want to become another statistic and therefore did whatever possible once again to satisfy my flesh and its desire to now "save face" by adding marriage to the equation.

The remaining chapters of this book will be used to dive deeper into these three things, as well as to highlight the other areas of deception used by the enemy to draw us away from the will of God for our lives concerning choosing a mate. Often times rather than wait for God, we will go out and find our own mates based upon our past experiences and knowledge, or lack thereof, and then we attempt to shove our choices in the face of God by asking Him to bless the messes we've gotten ourselves into.

Making A List
&
Checking It Twice

Chapter 8

"...After going through a gut wrenching break up and what appeared to be the end of the world with Daniel, a guy I'd met in my first year of high school, and raked over the coals by several others prior to him, (and all this occurring at the tender age of 14), I'd closed off my heart and swore to never allow myself to endure the pain I'd felt with him again. I'd made a mental note to self that it would be a miracle if I ever found or allowed myself to "love" again. This next guy would have to be a true present day knight in shining armor who'd sweep me off my feet by being all that Daniel was and more."

In following my story, as well as the story of many others, the man I married found me at a time in my life where I'd been recently wounded by the rejection and betrayal of a former mate as well as many of the other males I'd encountered, (including the perceived rejection and betrayal of my father). This rejection and betrayal caused me to build and hide myself behind a virtual wall; a wall that would be used to close everyone out as well as to hide myself behind. This wall was compiled of pain, prejudices, and checklist to follow before allowing anyone else into my heart.

The first to begin chipping away at this wall was the first to make me feel a sense of security. He immediately entered my life taking on the role of my protector. He was my knight in shining armor of sorts. His attempt to "protect me against the enemy in the papered ball war" immediately commanded my attention, and the manner in which he carried himself along with his style of dress was fresh and new to me, comparable only to that of my father, I was intrigued to say the very least.

What's on Your List?

So you've had a few failed relationships and now you've made up your mind that from now on you're going to weed out the bad apples early, and of course the best way to do that is to make a checklist. A list that will be cautiously and carefully reviewed every time someone comes along who may be interested in getting to know you better, however there is usually not as much caution and care for the compilation of said list.

-The lust of the flesh and eyes, are likely to play a huge role, by primarily addressing only the physical attributes we want in a mate.

- I only want a man who is tall, dark, and handsome.
- I want a man who is short and stocky.
- I want a man who is bald, long haired, green eyes, etc.

The list may also address the financial expectations we have of our mate.

- My man has to have enough money to take care of me and our children.

- I don't want to work for a living; I want to be a stay at home mom, so the man I meet has to be okay with the old school method.

- He has to make six figures and be able to buy me a nice home, car, jewelry etc.

Though I didn't know it at the time, I had a physical and financial expectation of the man I would marry as well, which was evident when I chose to fall head over heels in love with, and eventually marry Brandon. After carefully inspecting his physical attributes, they were eerily similar to those of my father, and their attitude in regard to the handling of women, finances, etc. were identical as well.

Aside from setting in place the attributes we want, we may even begin to compile a list of things that we vow to avoid in future relationships. Because I'd been in a relationship with Daniel and had several others who I'd become involved with in one way or another prior to Brandon, I'd made the decision to completely avoid any other guy unless he was able to compare in some way to Daniel. Better than that, even supersede the role that Daniel had once played in my life. I had yet to forgive for the pain I'd endured prior to Brandon and as a result, I'd become bitter.

The pride of life…

If we are not careful, our pride can get involved in our every thought and action when we have decided to defend and protect ourselves from others, rather than allow God to defend and protect us. We are likely operating in pride when we chose to avoid relationships with others or hold them to a preconceived set of standards often developed by hurt, bitterness, and un-forgiveness. In order to move on in any area of our lives we must address the pain we have experienced in our past. Bitterness and the inability to forgive others are like poison to relationships. They will cause one to develop an attitude of superiority towards their offender, and to become self-righteous as the offended will begin to point out and even keep record of any wrongs done by others.

As in my case, I'd carried over the bitterness and un-forgiveness I had from prior relationships and therefore made the first requirement on my list that this new person would need to be willing to put in the necessary work to break down the walls I'd built around my heart. I'd even decided to require that he was able to in some way or another match up to a mate from the past. He needed to display the qualities I'd discovered and enjoyed from the guy I'd dated before him, as well as be certain to not have the qualities that caused the breakdown of our relationship.

The pride that we develop during our upbringing affects our "list making" as well.

Because of how we were raised, we may knowingly or unknowingly require that our new mate can some way match up to, or have qualities that are in total opposition to those of our parents; or anyone who our parents may have chosen as mates. For instance if you have a mother or father who was controlling toward their mate or maybe even towards you, you may decide that in no way, shape or form will you ever allow yourself to be involved in a situation such as this.

Or perhaps you have a parent who is just the opposite and is a complete pushover in your eyes, and as a result you may adopt the same spirit, or take on a rebellious spirit instead, as a way of protecting yourself.

In summary if we're not careful, our past, the way someone dresses, and other physical characteristics, will begin to overshadow the more important and vital necessities of a successful relationship, which is unfortunate and shallow to say the least. After all, we never know what type of wrapping paper God will use for our gift. God may want us to experience the very emotional reaction we are attempting to avoid by creating these lists.

Now, in no way, am I attempting to say that we should not have any expectations or standards set when entering into a situation as important as choosing a mate, however we must ensure that our expectations are not fueled by past rejections, bitterness and prejudices, rather than the leading of the Holy Spirit.

Dressed For Success

Chapter 9

"…After leaving the assembly, I hadn't really thought too much about the encounter with B. After all, he was obviously older than me, which meant we probably wouldn't have any classes together, and besides that there was no way he hadn't already been claimed by the token beauty and captain of the cheer team I assumed. However I did run across him from time to time in the lunchroom and hallways, and when I did I tried my best to ensure that I'd cross every "t" and dot every "(i)" for the encounter. I'd begin by shellacking layers of lip gloss, dousing myself in perfume, and as if the already tight jeans that gave the appearance of being painted on weren't doing enough to advertise my curves, I'd be sure to accentuate the positive by adding a spine jerking switch to my walk when I knew he was behind me."

Now that I'd finally chosen to allow someone in, I'd begun to act and dress the part necessary, so that I'd be chosen by him as well. Because I felt inadequate in my own character, I chose to change the way I shopped for clothing, choosing only clothes that were revealing and certain to grab the attention of this man who I found to be out of my league. I no longer had the unsure, hesitant walk of the new girl at school when around him and instead had adopted an eye catching, head turning, switch to accompany my walk when around him.

I took no thought of what this actually meant, or to the fact that I was actually playing the role of a walking billboard; advertising myself in a way that would provoke any male to lust and sexual sin.
So here I am attempting to be chosen as a mate, but advertising myself as a set of lips, hips, and thighs instead.

What Are You Wearing, and Why?

We attract an audience with what we wear, and our clothing speaks as to how we view ourselves. Because I viewed myself as inadequate and not up to Brandon's standards, I felt it was necessary to rely on what I knew worked for me in the past. From the time I started to develop physically, I was often hit on by men of all ages. There was no limit to the things some of them would claim to do for and/ or to me, if given a chance because I was so "sexy and mature for my age" (sickening to think of it now that I'm older and realize the perversion behind this!)

Brandon had met the requirements of my checklist and now I felt I needed to put my best self forward in order to be eligible for him as well.

How about you?
How far outside of yourself are you willing to go for the attention of the opposite sex?

Do you rely on your lips, breast, hips, or thighs as an asset? And does it worry you that you may not be seen or acknowledged unless you make it a point to flaunt these body parts?

When we behave this way, we are inviting others to lust after us though somehow or another it is actually love we are truly seeking and expect to acquire.

There is often something about a person that draws us in, whether it is their confidence, and/ or a fun and flirtatious type of energy, or lack thereof, (seeing as how there are some that are drawn to a certain level of innocence,) all of which is displayed in our choice of clothing whether we realize it or not. These are only a couple examples, but I'm sure if you take some time and allow yourself to recall some of your past relationships and how they began, you may recognize some truth to this.

The lust of the flesh and the lust of the eyes are usually the driving forces behind choosing our mates before we get saved and allow God to assist us with the choosing.

Another important note to add is that when we dress, what we put on physically is only a small part of it all, because often times our natural appearance is used to display where we are spiritually.
Is your clothing speaking to your level of confidence or lack thereof?

Does what you have on represent you as someone who is seeking attention or one who is hoping to blend in the crowd and not be seen at all?

What type of spirit are you covered in?

Soul Mate

Chapter 10

"...Sure we had our problems, but we had "good" jobs, a house, a new car (for me) and even a conversion van (for him); and did I mention our dog Kiss and cat Heather? More importantly we were soul mates; we loved each other and had a family. Considering we'd never seen our parents interact for more than a few minutes at a time, let alone live together with all the fixings, we felt as if we had something really special. ."

In Brandon, I saw what I wanted in a mate, felt how I wanted to feel when around him, and would stop at nothing to live in that moment forever. Once our daughter was born and he'd made the decision to be in our lives, our relationship made a dramatic turn for the best! We were soon on the same page and shared the same mind about a lot of things especially when it came to raising Brionna. We'd slowly begun to gel well together. Our lives had found its niche, its routine of sorts. Eventually we'd gotten to the place where we could finish each other's sentences and even developed the ability to verbalize what the other was thinking from just a glance at each other. We were soul mates. He'd do whatever it took to make sure I was happy, and I would do the same for him.

The next step I'd taken after becoming pregnant and having our daughter was to leave my mother's home and move into my own place and from there into a place with him. I'd zipped right past God's order of things well before this and was only concerned once again about the *lust of my flesh, lust of my eyes and the pride of life.*

The lust of my flesh was briefly satisfied by having immediate access to him whenever I wanted to become involved with him whether it was in a sexual way or simply just the ability to talk to and see him every day. The lust of my eyes, by having the man I wanted and that perfect picture of a family to go along with it - made it almost like a dream come true, at least temporarily; and the pride of life was at its greatest when I combined the two. The fact that I had the man that I wanted, a family against all odds and statistics, including that of many of our friends and family, especially our own parents, eventually led to haughtiness. We were proud of the idea that we'd made the unselfish decision to raise our child together rather than in broken homes like we'd experienced.

As the Word tells us in *Proverbs 16:18, "Pride goes before destruction, a haughty spirit before a fall,"* the breakdown of our family proved this scripture to be accurate to say the least.

Soul Mate or Soul Tie?

How many times have you said or heard someone say, "It was love at first sight.

I know this is the one for me. I get butterflies when they're around, or my heart aches when they're not around.

We can talk about anything together.

We have so many things in common.

I have never felt this way about any other person etc. etc.; this has to be my soul mate!"

How true is this I wonder? Is it really possible to look at someone and instantly fall in LOVE with them?

Can we really know if someone is the one God has for us without taking the time out to ask the Lord, and more importantly take the time to wait and allow God to answer us!

What exactly are the "butterflies" we feel when someone we like is around, and the heartache when they're gone?

Does the ability to converse with someone of the opposite sex actually serve as an indication that you have truly discovered your mate?

After carefully considering the answers to these questions, it quickly became evident to me that the answers, and the term "soul mate" is more times than not, directly linked to none other than infatuation and lust. It deals primarily with feelings and emotions and often has nothing to do with what is best for us spiritually, nor does it line up with God's Word concerning love or relationships. Love in my opinion will take time to develop and nurture, whereas lust has more of an immediate effect on us and causes us to make rash decisions and often skews our view of things.

Things unfortunately tend to become a lot more problematic and only intensify once we have committed the sin of fornication with someone. Fornication binds the involved parties spiritually, thus creating a bond with them, and generating what is known as a "soul tie" to them. Though a soul tie does involve the connecting of souls, it has nothing to do with whether or not this is the mate God has "chosen" for you, or in other words, your soul mate.

Another important thing to note is that soul ties are in fact spiritually binding; and as a result will require deliverance in the spiritual realm before they can truly be broken.

The closest similarity to "soul mate" that I can find in my studies, would be the joining of two in marriage. The Bible describes this process as two becoming one.

The process of mating souls is hard work to say the very least. There will be many negative influences that'll come about in an effort to steal the desire once felt for one another and the sincerity of the vows exchanged. To kill the joy once felt in the relationship, and worse yet, destroy the hope and promises of a future together.

To sum things up, without the agreement and covenant sealed between God and the involved parties, the two may have a relationship with each other, likely to result in a soul tie with one another, rather than a soul mate.

What or Whom Are You Listening To?

Chapter 11

"…Of course we'd discuss marriage from time to time, but it wasn't something that either of us felt we needed to rush into. However with every reminder that we were "shacking," and every announcement of my friends and peers that they'd decided to take that next step and marry, I'd begin to feel inadequate and entertained the idea that maybe I was one of the 'cows giving out free milk and never to be purchased'…"

Shortly after moving in with each other we seemingly were bombarded with questions about our relationship, varying from, "Where did you two meet, to when are you two going to get married and have another child?"

The constant pressure from the latter question weighed heavily on me. I'd begin to see others around us getting married and would instantly begin to question our love and commitment to one another. Or I'd hear someone say the infamous line that no single woman ever wants to hear, "A man isn't ever going to buy the cow if you continue to give him the milk for free," With that, the nagging and witchcraft began!

What Are You Listening To?

What does your IPOD or MP3 playlist look like? It is often said that our youth learn violent or inappropriate behaviors from television shows, movies, the lyrics of rap music, and even video games; which may be true. However I find that as adults, we have allowed ourselves to be overly influenced by television and movies, lyrics of "love" songs, and though we may not play video games, we have magazines and talk shows littered with the latest "Top 10 ways to catch a mate" and various other "games" we play with the opposite sex.

It is unfortunate, but true that celebrities have some of the highest divorce rates, yet we aim to model our relationships after the roles they play on videos and in films. We purchase magazines and dissect word for word their tips on love and relationships. Later we find the same magazine featuring the fall of this very relationship, as the cover story only months later; mind boggling to say the least.

Not only are we intrigued by the lifestyles of celebrities, but we allow ourselves to become mesmerized and even captivated by the lyrics to the songs they sing.

If the hottest new rap artist on the charts says, "You know she loves you when she buys you candy and sends smiley faced texts," surely that must be what he will look for when evaluating his relationship.

If the number one R&B song says, "he only loves you if he looks into your eyes and holds you tight," certainly the man you're dating needs to start looking and holding to make it official.

The videos and movies we watch paint the picture of love as a glance across the room, or a bouquet of flowers sent. All may be intriguing in the beginning of a relationship. However lust is more likely to be intriguing, whereas love is birthed through true friendship, intimacy and courtship.

Who Are You Listening To?

There is usually a constant barrage of influences from the family and friends of individuals who are single. Holidays and family gatherings become torturous as the attack begins as soon as you enter the gathering… alone…again!

"When you gone find yourself somebody?

When you gone get married and have some children?"

For those that are single and *saved*, the questions and comments posed may be slightly different,

"You still waiting on God to send your mate?

You better come and go out with us to the club sometimes.

You ain't ever gone find nobody sitting around the house, 'waiting on God'!"

All this and you have yet to make your round of hugs and hellos, let alone remove your coat.

Or maybe you *are* in a relationship and these same influences are encouraging you to leave your mate for one reason or another. If a woman, you may have someone tell you that she is too needy or clingy.

She seems like she's trying to change you or she seems like she's the type that'll hurt you.

If it's a man you are introducing, the input may be the same as well as he can't provide for you with that job.

He doesn't seem like the marrying kind, he'll just be stringing you along forever.

Then there's the pro marriage group that feels it's their duty to bring the subject up in every possible occasion… but no pressure right? After all it *is* the right thing to do, isn't it? That's what I found myself surrounded by before Brandon and I married, and when it wasn't them, it was the resounding message I'd hear when going to church or on the Christian programming I'd watch on television. Or at least that's what I thought the message from God to the two of us was. However I now know that though God may actually give you a vision or a Word that He is calling us to a "venture" or new thing, it doesn't mean it is the right time for us.

 Often times we move out of season, and as a result ruin the blessing God has for us.

Just Put a Ring on It

Chapter 12

…Our late night pillow talk sessions about one day getting married, having more children, and buying our dream home, became "nigga you Don't think we about to be having sex and laying up and we not married right? You need to quit talking about it and be about it! We ain't gone be shacking up and living in sin for life! I mean how long you think I'm gone live in this neighborhood, I'm ready to move, I want a baby", and so on and so on. He'd soon become regularly subjected to a full scale nagging session packed with rejection and manipulation, which became the catalyst, and unfortunate chain of events leading to me getting what I wanted, the proposal, the ring, and finally his last name, some courtship huh?"

Often times, we rush into marriages as if we were children at Christmas time: super excited about the big pretty bow and elaborate wrapping paper. With huge smiles and gleaming eyes, we may shake it a little hoping to get a hint of what's inside. When that loses its excitement, we tear off into it, no longer wowed by its wrapping and bow. Before long it's in our hands, but usually there are at least one or two more layers to fight through before we are able to play with our new toy. Finally we have the toy right where we want it and we're off to play with it. The instruction manual is tossed off to the side and nearly thrown out, before we realize we have no clue what we have in our hands, nor do we know what to do with it.

The same was true in my relationship with my husband. I'd used several tactics to "shake him up" in an effort to see what was really going on in his mind and heart regarding our relationship. I'd gotten past his style of dress and a few of the walls he had up due to past hurt and rejection and now I had him in my hands. I thought surely I know what to do with him and was ready to have him as my husband and I his wife. The instruction manual, being the Word of God, should have been my "go to," on "how to," however it was never even considered, and just as with any other gift, without the proper instruction, we are likely to get frustrated when it doesn't work as we expected it to and may even destroy it as a result.

I now know that the problems that destroyed our marriage were always there. Somehow I managed to fool myself into believing that the marriage we'd entered would be the remedy for our problems. After all, the only sin was the fornication we were committing by having premarital sex right… Not so!

Fornication is about falling prey to the enemy who sends a spirit of lust and sexual sin as a method of destroying the people of God. What I had not realized is I'd chosen to have sex with B because I was in a desperate and rejected place. I was desperate to have someone in my life that would love me and give me attention; someone who would fill my emptiness and provide some escape from the loneliness I felt for years. I won't say that I never had sexual desires, as humans the desire to be intimate is natural, but I will say that I would've been content without it. My decision to begin a sexual relationship with B was based on the urgency I felt to do any and everything he requested of me so that he would not leave me. Without being too graphic, in an act of desperation, I brought myself to offer an alternative method of pleasing him when I recognized the disappointment he felt as I denied him the act of sex. I was not able to give him myself completely on that day, but I certainly did all that I could to display my willingness to please him in any way possible.

I now see that this one act of desperation became the thread of our relationship. No matter what it would require of me mentally, physically, sexually, emotionally and eventually even spiritually, I was willing to sacrifice my needs for his. I would always place the desire I had for his happiness ahead of my own happiness. I lusted after the "love" that he'd give me for sacrificing my desires for his, and he lusted after the gratification of his flesh, with which I was able to accommodate him.

Just 'Cause We Like "It" Does Not Mean Put a Ring on It!

"If you like it …put a ring on it." Many of us have used this phrase and yeah, it may sound good, but in this saying, lays a trap designed for our fall!

A ring signifies many things, but it doesn't symbolize the end of all problems and resolution of all sins. It doesn't symbolize anything but a piece of jewelry when the relationship is void of love, honor and respect… you know all those lovely things we vow to have for one another on the wedding day.

I can still remember the day I received my engagement ring, not because it was one of those extra "romantic" proposal moments we often see on television, but because it was when I least expected it. He presented it to me as I sat in the company of our daughter, his mother and a few other family members. Can't remember much of his proposal, because we were all shouting in excitement and amazement, however, I can clearly recall the end where he asked me, "Okay, now you can remove and throw out that "thing" you have on your finger right?"

"That thing" that he spoke of was a part of my grand scheme. Because he had taken too long (in my opinion) to produce a ring as promised, I decided I'd go myself and purchase a ring. I was "engaged" and I felt that the world needed to know it. Now that I am able to look back on things, I wonder if it was my way of reminding B and I of our promise to marry, more so than informing the world of anything. So sad!

The lust of my flesh, lust of my eyes and my pride, had taken over yet again, and as we often do with our impatient ways, I'd ever so casually stripped B of his manhood and stepped in as the enabler I was to "fix" things for him.

What is Your Motivation?

If you are in a relationship and find yourself gawking in the window of every jewelry store for the "perfect" ring, throwing hints and temper tantrums in an effort to rush your mate into marriage, examine your heart to find out why. Allow God to show you what your motives actually are.

Is sex your motivation?
Is it security?
Is it completion?

Many have the false idea that marriage means endless sex with God's approval. "If we just go ahead and get married we can have sex and God will be okay with it then," we think. – Lust of the flesh at its best or should I say its worst.
Because we decide to put a "ring" on lust, doesn't mean it pleases God, He knows our motives and judges us accordingly.

If your motivation is not sex, maybe it's because you have a false sense that marriage will provide security or completion for you. It took a while for me to learn this lesson but God is the only One that can bring true security and completion into our lives. Until we learn that, He will open our eyes in an effort to allow us to see what and who we are choosing over Him. He will reveal to us just how unstable the "gods" we chose to substitute for Him are, and how they are sure to fail us in our time of need.

Better a Piece Than None at All

Chapter 13

It was almost immediate the change that began to take place in our lives. I had become the nagging woman who I'm sure B would've traded for that corner of the roof mentioned in the book of Proverbs, *("better to live on a corner of the roof than share a house with a quarrelsome wife" Proverbs 25:24,)* constantly nagging and using every bit of power I had over him. I wanted to have my way and would stop at nothing to get it. I'd withhold sex, give him the silent treatment for days at a time, and would continually threaten to leave him if he would not carry out his promise to marry me. All of which were forms of witchcraft, an attempt to have control over my life as well as control of his, which we all know is sure to breed rebellion, and it did. He rebelled against anything to do with marriage for a long time and though he finally went along with my request, it was evident by his actions that the rebellion continued throughout the majority of our marriage.

Only God knows the truth of the behaviors and activities he'd taken part in from day one of our relationship, but everything slowly began to be exposed. The cheating, the lies, the mismanagement of our joint accounts, all of these actions and more were thrown in my face and seemingly at once. As I think of it now, it's interesting that the careless way in which each of these secrets were revealed, may have been his way of exposing himself as a form of rebellion against me and my demands of him. This may have also been the Lord exposing to me the truth and the severity of the situation I was getting myself into. However I chose to ignore these signs and except B's deceptive responses when confronted with the issues. I'd even make the excuse that these were only ways in which the devil was attempting to destroy our plans to finally commit to one another in marriage. I made the decision to turn a blind eye to the truth and deafened ear as well. In making a conscious decision to ignore the truth, I'd clearly chosen my lust for marriage over truth. There was not much else that mattered to me at this point. I was willing to accept anything that he'd do or say as long as I was able to get what I wanted. Truth, trust, faithfulness, or any of the expected requirements for a successful marriage, no longer meant anything. I was on a mission to "please God," we had an already made family and not only that, we loved each other, and in my opinion that was all we would need.

The Counterfeit

Chapter 14

We were confused and tricked by the enemy which was not hard to do considering neither of us had truly experienced the love of others and more importantly, the love of Christ. It felt right to us. So we went head first into this thing without seeking God, without listening to the Spirit that spoke to us even as sinners. I can even recall believing that the signs and feelings that I'd experienced that urged me not to marry but to remove myself from the relationship were from the devil.

Surely God has not sent this thing - whether it was a word of wisdom from one of my favorite television evangelists, or even the actual revelation of truth pertaining to lies and secrets that were exposed just days before and even on the day of our vow exchange. I was certain that these turn of events were all the workings of the devil sent to hinder us from doing what God was requiring of us. I now know that the devil, which is the father of lies and chooses only to deceive the people of God, would never opt to reveal truth to me. Now, had the things that had come about been lies, I'd have every right to believe that it was the enemy attempting to hinder us from marrying, however they were true. I now believe that my Father was revealing these things to me in an effort to get me to make a wiser choice, and/or to allow me to see exactly what I was getting myself into and preparing me for the road ahead. Rather than listen, I chose once again out of desperation and rejection to grasp and hold on for dear life onto deception. I allowed myself to be lead away captive by the desires of my flesh, rather than be led by the Spirit of God. Never taking even a moment to inquire of The Lord, an elder, or for that matter even my fiancé to see what our next move should be.

Should we continue on, or turn away and wait for Wisdom to guide us?

Our relationship was solely based on doing only what was necessary to keep the other around so that our desires would be met. It was a self -seeking love; An impatient, unkind, envious, haughty, rude, self-seeking love, and as we read in the book of Corinthians Chapter 13, these are the primary examples given for what love should NOT look or feel like.

Lust; Loves Counterfeit

When we are operating solely in our flesh nature, we rely upon our feelings and emotions more so than the Spirit of God, and therefore open ourselves up to deception and counterfeits. Lust is love's counterfeit. It may look similar to love, but that is only true when we use the world's standards to compare the two. We have all seen a teller or store clerk at one time or another take a bill of currency, mark it and hold it up into the light to check for authenticity. It's amazing how true the same is for authenticating love. Because God is love and the Creator of love, we should be able to "hold love up to the Light of His Word" and see His Face. The counterfeit will not be able to produce the same "markings" when held up to the Light! It will not be able to display the characteristics the Bible has given us for love.

Loves is

Chapter 15

"Love is patient, love is kind. It does not envy, it does not boast, it is not proud. It is not rude, it is not self-seeking, it is not easily angered, it keeps no record of wrongs. Love
does not delight in evil but rejoices with the truth. It always protects, always trusts, always hopes, always perseveres. Love never fails..."

1 Corinthians 13:4-8 (NIV)

Love is PATIENT!
Are you patient with your significant other, and vice versa?

Love is KIND!
Are you kind to one another, even when it's hard?

Love KEEPS NO RECORD OF WRONGS!
Are you constantly bringing up what your mate or others have done to wrong you?

I challenge you to get to know what, better yet Who Love is!

Next, examine yourself and your relationships.

Use the Word of God to help you to gauge whether "he loves you, or loves you not," and vice versa!

God is Love

Chapter 16

Whoever does not love does not know God, because God is love.

1 John 4:8 (NIV)

God is love, and as read in I Corinthians Chapter 13, Love does not delight in evil but rejoices with the truth. God doesn't experience joy when we accept and fall prey to the spirit of lust, thus denying His Spirit. Nor does He delight in our marriages falling apart. He actually says in Malachi Chapter 3 that He hates divorce and marital separation. However when these things occur God knows that they are acts that are not unto death. Once truth is revealed, God is a restorer and delights in the reconciliation of marriage, when the necessary steps are taken to go forth in His way and the truth of His Word.

Love always protects and therefore God always looks out for His children and desires that we have His best. He will not allow us to be fooled by the devices of the enemy. He will send others to speak truth and He will reveal it to us in His Word. Though it may not be said in the right spirit, He may even choose your spouse to speak truth.

 I can recall several times during my separation with my husband becoming angry and yelling, "You don't love me and you never did. It's always all about you!" Wow, this was certainly the truth; my husband had not yet learned to love me, just as I hadn't learned to love him, and we were definitely happiest when things were all about us!

One good thing is, when we give our lives over to Christ, we learn of Him and begin to take on His nature. We are also permitted to take on His mind. As we do this, we learn to trust God with our hearts and our marriages. We learn to hope for God's best and the acquiring of His promises for our lives and marriages and we learn to persevere during the waiting period. God is more than able to restore our broken relationships and marriages when we have faith in, and trust Him to do so. However we must allow our love and obedience to Him to rebuild the foundations of our marriages.

Love Must Be The Foundation

Chapter 17

The foundation of our marriage was not what God requires, hence the break down and ultimate act of divorce. Lust is fickle and thus does not have the resilience necessary for the institution of marriage. Marriage is a covenant vow exchange in which both parties involved must first agree to LOVE one another. It is a covenant spoken before God and God will hold us accountable to this vow. He is not concerned with when we acquire the knowledge of this accountability, though I'm sure He would prefer us to be informed prior to marriage. His Word has said that the people of God perish because of their lack of knowledge, and the same is true for marriages. When we enter into these covenant agreements without the knowledge of the magnitude of this decision, we are not exempt from the accountability and expectations of God for us to carry out all that we have vowed.

Tips To Love By

Chapter 18

-We must allow Love to heal and restore our broken areas.

Past hurts and rejections cause us to "make lists" for the people in your life to follow.
Allow God's Word to "make the list." He will show you what the qualifications are and what you should be looking for when deciding to date or court for marriage.

Our inability to see ourselves as God sees us causes us to rely on worldly methods of acquiring a mate, ("dressing for success,") being one of them.

When we rely on God for our every decision, He will show us how to spiritually dress for success in every area of our lives.

-The idea of finding a "soul mate," or finding someone and instantly falling head over heels for them and it actually being love, rather than lust is possible I'm sure, but highly unlikely.

Examine those feelings closely and allow the Word of God to reveal what type of mate you've stumbled upon.

-It is important that we are not more focused on pleasing, competing with, or mimicking others more so than God.

Be careful and choose wisely when deciding "who or what you listen to!"

Again, allow God to be your counselor!

Getting married is an agreement that involves three! It is a decision to enter into a covenant relationship with not only your mate, but with God as well.

Examine what the motivation is, behind your decision to marry.

Do you feel as if "putting a ring on it," would please God and be the answer to all your relationship problems?

Marriage does not cancel out the sin of lust!

-Love has been said to be "blind," but love is certainly not dumb!

God has a way of revealing truth to us and we have to want to see and hear the truth when He shows us! No matter the immediate pain it may cause, if we don't confront it when He reveals it, it will only resurface and cause greater pain later!

-Better to have an internal Peace than an external Piece!

It is always better to have none at all and have peace, than it is to have "a piece" of a relationship to pacify our flesh.

-GOD IS LOVE and love must be the foundation of our relationships!

Because lust is fickle, it is dangerous and nearly impossible to build a successful relationship on a foundation of lust.

-Allow the Light of God's Word to discover love and expose lust; the counterfeit!

If your story is anything like ours, you may find yourself guilty of falling in lust, assuming that you'd fallen in love and now you're wondering what to do. My best advice would be that you take a moment alone with yourself and God.

In this moment:

You must allow yourself to receive and embrace truth!

Forgive yourself!

Forgive your significant other!

Let go as God leads!

Press on! Allowing God to carry you through this place, and into the new place He has for you!

Get to know Love!

Only Love can teach us to love!

Anything outside of Him is sure to be none other than loves counterfeit.

Author Bio

LaWanda Montgomery was born, raised and currently resides in Michigan, along with her daughter LaShara. She is a part of the leadership team at her church, Greater Works Family Ministries of Detroit and makes a living as an entrepreneur. In 2011, her passion for Massage Therapy and business management merged and she became the Owner and Operator of "A Way of Escape," a Mobile Massage and Spa Treatment Company also in Michigan. She recently rediscovered her love for writing resulting in "He Loves Me, He Loves Me NOT" and has plans to write more in the upcoming future.

Other books that deal with Lust,
Love & Relationships
by
Destiny House Publishing

Marriage For A Lifetime

When the Vow

BREAKS

Discover How You Can Restore
Hope & Healing in Your Marriage

Oscar & Crystal Jones

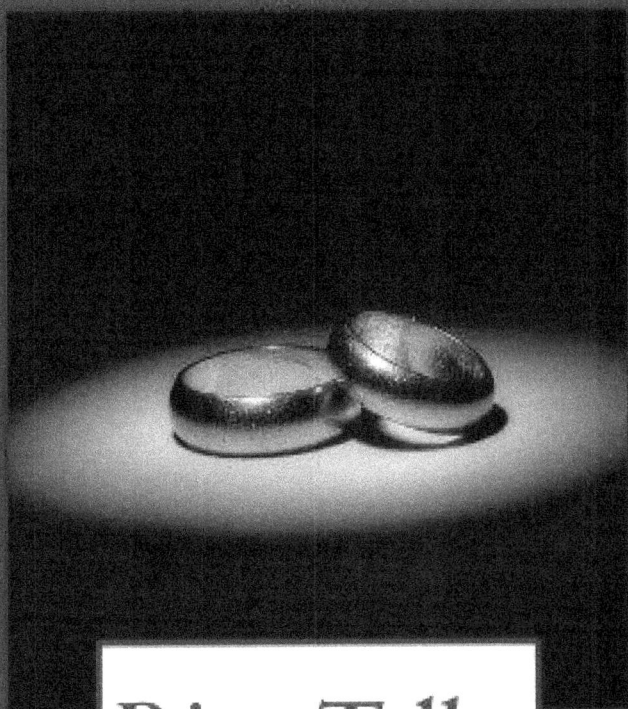

Ring Talks

A Guide to Husband-Wife Meetings

Oscar &
Crystal Jones

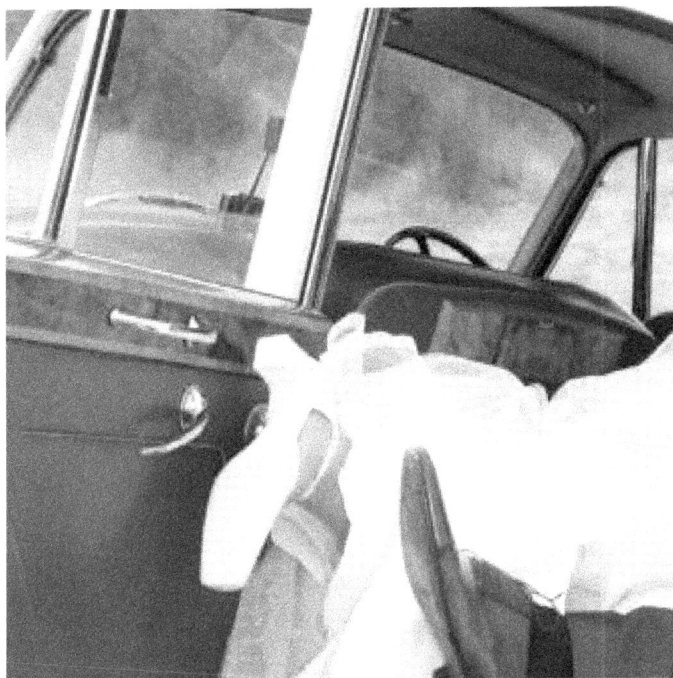

THE NEWLYWED HANDBOOK

Oscar & Crystal Jones

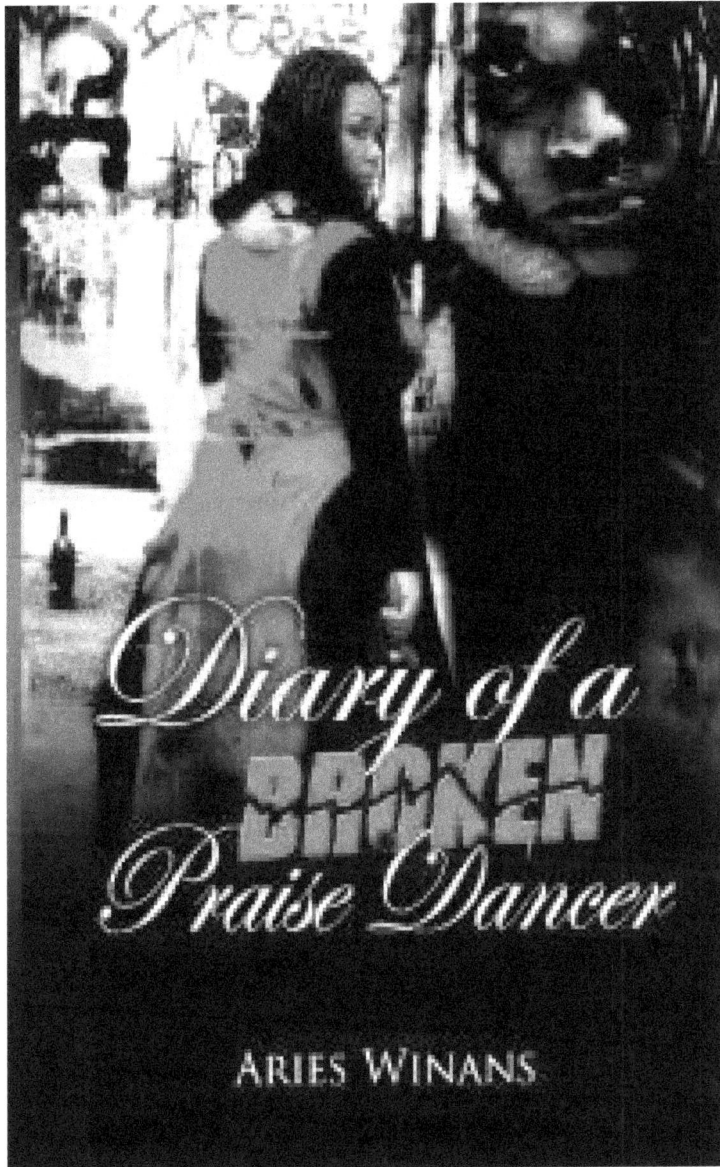

Diary of a BROKEN Praise Dancer

ARIES WINANS

Copyrighted Material
CRYSTAL JONES
I WANT A HUSBAND, TOO
Copyrighted Material

Contact Us

Destiny House Publishing
P.O. Box 19774
Detroit, MI 48219
BY PHONE:
888.890.9455
service@destinyhousepublishing.com

www.ingramcontent.com/pod-product-compliance
Lightning Source LLC
Chambersburg PA
CBHW060806050426
42449CB00008B/1569